ZEBRAS

Sandie Lee Books

Zebras

The zebra is a horse-like animal that is in the African equidae family. However, unlike horses, the zebra has never been domesticated (tamed). There are 3 species of the zebra; the Common zebra, the Mountain zebra and the Grevy's zebra. The entire zebra species dates back about 4 million years ago. The zebra is a fascinating animal, so let's explore its world a little further. Read on to discover what this animal eats, its defense and so much more.

Where in the World?

Did you know the zebra only lives in Africa? Herds of this animal like to live in various areas of Africa. They can be found on savannas, woodlands, grasslands, thorny scrublands, mountainous areas, as well as the coastal hills. Ngorongoro Crater in Tanzania has a large population of the zebra.

The Body of a Zebra

Did you know the body of a zebra is like a horse? The zebra has four slender legs with a hoof on each one. It has a large head with a long snout. Its eyes are on the side of its head. The mane and tail of the zebra has long hair. The zebra's ears usually stand straight up on its head.

The Size of the Zebra

Did you know the zebra is a bit smaller than a normal-sized horse? The zebra can range in size from 3.5 feet to 5 feet tall at the shoulder. Depending on the species, this animal can weigh anywhere from 440 pounds all the way up to 990 pounds.

The Zebra's Stripes

Did you know the stripes on a zebra are all uniquely patterned? Like our fingerprints, each zebra has its own special pattern of stripes. These stripes act as camouflage for the zebra when it is in a large group - it is hard to tell where one zebra starts and the other ends.

What a Zebra Eats

Did you know the main diet of the zebra is grass? This animal will also dine on leaves, bark, buds, fruit and roots. It will graze most of the day in a large herd. The zebra uses its sharp front teeth to bite the grass from the ground. The back teeth are used to crush and ground the food.

The Zebra's Defense

Did you know the zebra uses its stripes as a defense? Large cats will hunt the zebra. However, when it is in a large group (and all the stripes are mixing together) the cat gets confused and can't pinpoint just one. Zebra will also kick out with its powerful back legs.

The Zebra as Prey

Did you know the zebra is hunted by many animals? The zebra has a number of different predators. Lions, leopards, cheetahs, African dogs and hyenas will all hunt this animal. Man will also hunt the zebra for sport and for its skin. The loss of the zebra's habitat is also posing a threat to these amazing creatures.

Zebra Talk

Did you know the zebra can make sounds? Zebras will communicate with high pitched barks and whinnying. Some zebras will make a mule-like braying sound. The zebra's ears will also say a lot about its mood. Erect ears can mean calm, tense or friendly. A frightened zebra's ears will be pushed forward and when its angry, the ears are pulled backward.

The Zebra Mom

Did you know, like a horse, the female zebra is called a mare? The female zebra is ready to have young at 3 years-old. Once pregnant, the mare will give birth to one baby every 12 months. She will nurse her baby until it is a year-old. The mother zebra protects her baby.

The Baby Zebra

Did you know baby zebras can stand shortly after birth? Baby zebras are called foals. They can stand, walk and suckle from their mother very quickly after they are born. This helps keep them safe from predators. The foal is also born white with brown stripes. The stripes will darken to black as the foal ages.

Zebras on the Move

Did you know the zebra can run up to 35 miles-per-hour? Zebras are constantly on the move. They do this to find fresh grass and water sources. The zebra will also make long journeys called, migration. This is to find better feeding grounds. These herds can consist of thousands of individual zebras.

Life of a Zebra

Did you know the zebra can live to be 25 years-old in the wild? Healthy zebras (if left alone) can live to be quite old. The zebra is social and will groom another zebra. It does this by gently biting at its fur. Zebras will stay among its family members in a large herd. The family will be made up of one male, several females and their young.

The Grevy's Zebra

This species of zebra is the largest of them all. It stands 5.5 feet tall at the shoulder and can weigh a whopping 990 pounds! It can be found in northern Kenya and southern and eastern Ethiopia. Due to poaching and habitat loss, the Grevy's zebra is highly endangered.

The Mountain Zebra

This zebra can be found on the slopes and plateaus of the mountains in Africa. It looks different from other species because of an extra flap of skin on its throat. This is called a, dewlap. The mountain zebra is now on the endangered list. This is due to extensive hunting of the animal for its skin. Habitat loss is also harming this species of the zebra.

Quiz

Question 1: What is one of the 3 species of the zebra called?

Answer 1: The common zebra, the mountain zebra or the Grevy's zebra

Question 2: Where is the only place on Earth the zebra can be found?

Answer 2: Africa

Question 3: Just like our fingerprints, what is unique about each zebra's stripes?

Answer 3: No two patterns are the same

Question 4: When a zebra's ears are standing straight up, what does this tell us?

Answer 4: The zebra may be calm, tense or being friendly

Question 5: How does a zebra groom another zebra?

Answer 5: By gently biting its fur

Thank you for checking out another addition from Sandie Lee Books! Make sure to check out Amazon.com for many other great titles.

www.ingramcontent.com/pod-product-compliance
Lightning Source LLC
Chambersburg PA
CBHW050803290526
45792CB00008B/2303